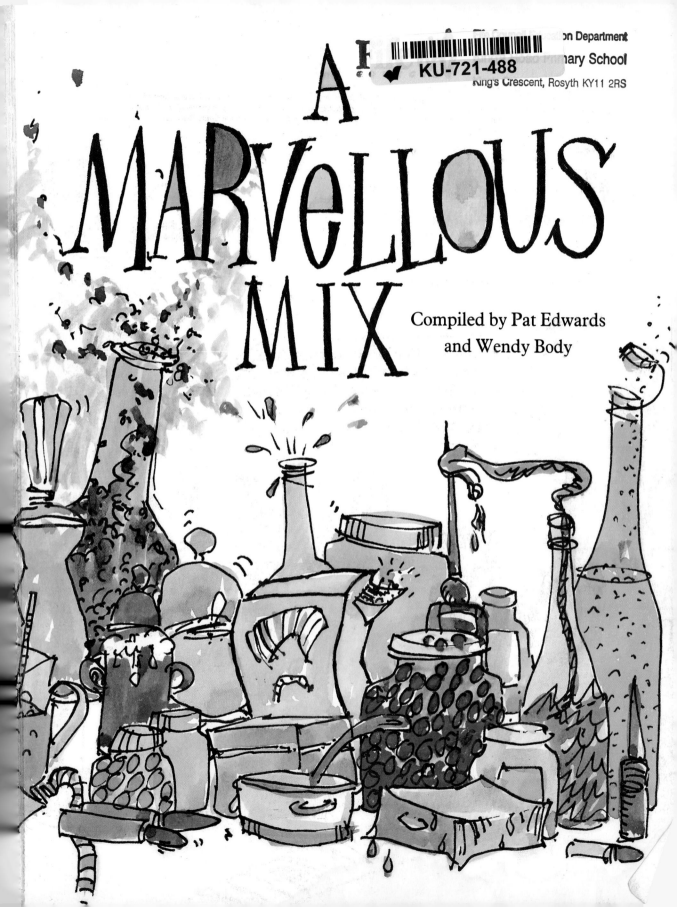

A MARVELLOUS MIX

Compiled by Pat Edwards
and Wendy Body

Acknowledgements

We are grateful to the following for permission to reproduce copyright material: the author's agents for the story 'A Postcard from the Stars' by Brian Ball from *Frank and Molly Muir's Big Dipper* compiled by Frank and Molly Muir (pub. Heinemann); the author's agent for the story 'Marvellous Medicine No.4, from *George's Marvellous Medicine* by Roald Dahl © Roald Dahl (pub. Jonathan Cape & Penguin); Hodder & Stoughton Ltd for the story 'Higgledy-Piggledy and Topsy-Turvy' from *Folk Tales For Reading and Telling* by Leila Berg (pub. Hodder & Stoughton Ltd); the author, Morris Lurie for his story 'The Training of a Champion' from *The 27th Annual African Hippopotamus Race* by Morris Lurie; Penguin Books Ltd for the poem 'Poor Doris' from *Wry Rhymes for Troublesome Times* by Max Fatchen (Kestrel Books 1983) Copyright © Max Fatchen 1983 and the story 'Lizzie Dripping and The Witch' from *Lizzie Dripping* by Helen Cresswell (Puffin Books 1984) Copyright © Helen Cresswell 1973. Pages 16–17 were written by Debbie Fox. Page 38 was written by Bill Boyle.

We are grateful to the following for permission to reproduce photograph: Camera Press, page 15 (photo: L. Cherrault/H. Jemmet).

Illustrators include: Bettina Guthridge pp. 4–12; 62–4; Brett Colquhoun p. 13; Shelagh McNicholas pp. 14–15; Antonia Enthoven pp. 16–17; Gordon Fichett pp. 18–25; Bryna Waldman pp. 26–38; Gaston Vanzet pp. 39–51; Cindy Hunnam pp. 52–9; Alan Jane pp. 60–1.

Contents

George Kranky has the nastiest old grandmother in the world. She's also fearfully bossy. So George decides to make Grandma some medicine so fierce and so fantastic it will either cure her completely or blow off the top of her head. The trouble is that the medicine turns Grandma into a giant — a huge, skinny, bossy giant. George uses up the rest of the mixture on the farm animals, who all grow into giants too. Mr Kranky is very excited and asks George to make some more, but George can't quite get it right. He tries again and again. Now he's about to get a hen to sample his . . .

Marvellous Medicine No 4

George knelt down and held out the spoon with the new medicine in it. "Chick-chick," he said. "Try some of this."

The brown hen walked over and looked at the spoon. Then it went *peck*.

"*Owch!*" it said. Then a funny whistling noise came out of its beak.

"Watch it grow!" shouted Mr Kranky.

"Don't be too sure," said Mrs Kranky. "Why is it whistling like that?"

"Keep quiet, woman!" cried Mr Kranky. "Give it a chance!"

They stood there staring at the brown hen.

"It's getting smaller," George said. "Look at it, dad. It's shrinking."

And indeed it was. In less than a minute, the hen had shrunk so much it was no bigger than a new-hatched chick. It looked ridiculous.

"There's still something you've left out," Mr Kranky said.

"I can't think what it could be," George said.

"Give it up," Mrs Kranky said. "Pack it in. You'll never get it right."

Mr Kranky looked very forlorn.

George looked pretty fed up, too. He was still kneeling on the ground with the spoon in one hand and the cup full of medicine in the other. The ridiculous tiny brown hen was walking slowly away.

At that point, Grandma came striding into the yard. From her enormous height, she glared down at the three people below her and she shouted, "What's going on around here? Why hasn't anyone brought me my morning cup of tea? It's bad enough having to sleep in the yard with the rats and mice but I'll be blowed if I'm going to starve as well! No tea! No eggs and bacon! No buttered toast!"

"I'm sorry, mother," Mrs Kranky said. "We've been terribly busy. I'll get you something right away."

"Let George get it, the lazy little brute!" Grandma shouted.

Just then, the old woman spotted the cup in George's hand. She bent down and peered into it. She saw that it was full of brown liquid. It looked very much like tea. "Ho-ho!" she cried. "Ha-ha! So that's your little game, is it! You look after yourself all right, don't you! You make quite sure *you've* got a nice cup of morning tea! But you didn't think to bring one to your poor old Grandma! I always knew you were a selfish pig!"

6

"No, Grandma," George said. "This isn't . . ."

"Don't lie to me, boy!" the enormous old hag shouted. "Pass it up here this minute!"

"No!" cried Mrs Kranky. "No, mother, don't! That's not for you!"

"Now *you're* against me, too!" shouted Grandma. "My own daughter trying to stop me having my breakfast! Trying to starve me out!"

Mr Kranky looked up at the horrid old woman and he smiled sweetly. "Of course it's for you, Grandma," he said. "You take it and drink it while it's nice and hot."

"Don't think I won't," Grandma said, bending down from her great height and reaching out a huge horny hand for the cup. "Hand it over, George."

"No, no, Grandma!" George cried out, pulling the cup away. "You mustn't! You're not to have it!"

"Give it to me, boy!" yelled Grandma.

"Don't!" cried Mrs Kranky. "That's George's Marvellous . . ."

"Everything's George's round here!" shouted Grandma. "George's this, George's that! I'm fed up with it!"

7

She snatched the cup out of little George's hand and carried it high up out of reach.

"Drink it up, Grandma," Mr Kranky said, grinning hugely. "Lovely tea."

"No!" the other two cried. "No, no, no!"

But it was too late. The ancient beanpole had already put the cup to her lips, and in one gulp she swallowed everything that was in it.

"Mother!" wailed Mrs Kranky. "You've just drunk fifty doses of George's Marvellous Medicine Number Four and look what one tiny spoonful did to that little old brown hen!" But Grandma didn't even hear her. Great clouds of steam were already pouring out of her mouth and she was beginning to whistle.

"This is going to be interesting,"
Mr Kranky said, still grinning.

"Now you've done it!" cried
Mrs Kranky, glaring at her husband.
"You've cooked the old girl's goose!"

"I didn't do anything," Mr Kranky said.

"Oh, yes you did! You told her to drink it!"

A tremendous hissing sound was coming from above
their heads. Steam was shooting out of Grandma's
mouth and nose and ears and whistling as it came.

"She'll feel better after she's let off a bit of steam,"
Mr Kranky said.

"She's going to blow up!" Mrs Kranky wailed.
"Her boiler's going to burst!"

"Stand clear," Mr Kranky said.

George was quite alarmed. He stood up and ran back a few paces. The jets of white steam kept squirting out of the skinny old hag's head, and the whistling was so high and shrill it hurt the ears.

"Call the fire-brigade!" cried Mrs Kranky. "Call the police! Man the hose-pipes!"

"Too late," said Mr Kranky, looking pleased.

"Grandma!" shrieked Mrs Kranky. "Mother! Run to the drinking-trough and put your head under the water!"

But even as she spoke, the whistling suddenly stopped and the steam disappeared. That was when Grandma began to get smaller. She had started off with her head as high as the roof of the house, but now she was coming down fast.

"Watch this, George!" Mr Kranky shouted, hopping around the yard and flapping his arms. "Watch what happens when someone's had fifty spoonfuls instead of one!"

Very soon, Grandma was back to normal height.

"Stop!" cried Mrs Kranky. "That's just right."

But she didn't stop. Smaller and smaller she got . . . down and down she went. In another half minute she was no bigger than a bottle of lemonade.

"How d'you feel, mother?" asked Mrs Kranky anxiously.

Grandma's tiny face still bore the same foul and furious expression it always had. Her eyes, no bigger now than little keyholes, were blazing with anger. "How do I *feel*?" she yelled. "How d'you *think* I feel? How would *you* feel if you'd been a glorious giant a minute ago and suddenly you're a miserable midget?"

"She's still going!" shouted Mr Kranky gleefully. "She's still getting smaller!"

And by golly, she was.

When she was no bigger than a cigarette, Mrs Kranky made a grab for her. She held her in her hands and she cried, "How do I stop her getting smaller still?"

"You can't," said Mr Kranky. "She's had fifty times the right amount."

"I *must* stop her!" Mrs Kranky wailed. "I can hardly see her as it is!"

"Catch hold of each end and pull," Mr Kranky said.

By then, Grandma was the size of a matchstick and still shrinking fast.

A moment later, she was no bigger than a pin . . .

then a pumpkin seed . . .

then . . . then . . .

"Where is she?" cried Mrs Kranky. "I've lost her!"

"Hooray," said Mr Kranky.

"She's gone! She's disappeared completely!" cried Mrs Kranky.

"That's what happens to you if you're grumpy and bad-tempered," said Mr Kranky. "Great medicine of yours, George."

George didn't know what to think.

Roald Dahl
Illustrated by Bettina Guthridge

But no medicine could help...

Poor Doris

Poor Doris, so terribly tender
Was somehow caught up in a blender.
It beat her to pulp
And well you might gulp.
The chances are slim that they'll mend her.

13

Max Fatchen.

Roald Dahl has written lots of stories for adults. Many of them have been adapted for television.

Some children probably know him best for his children's books.

Have you read any of these?

Roald Dahl in his greenhouse

FOLKLORE

For many years people have used things from nature to help them look and feel better. Folklore really means what people know and what they believe. People talked to each other and their ideas spread. Some of the remedies they used may seem very strange, but some may still be used today.

People had many different ideas on how to get rid of warts

Some people rubbed their warts with a radish, some rubbed them with the juice of the marigold flower and some found a black slug and rubbed the wart with that!

Other people believed that the best cure for warts was to steal a piece of beef. They rubbed the wart with the piece of beef and then buried the beef. Then the wart would disappear.

Have you ever been stung by a nettle?

One remedy that people still use today is to rub the sting with a dock leaf. In Ireland people used to sing a rhyme as they rubbed the dock leaves onto the sting:

Dock in, dock in, in and out,
Take the sting of the nettle out.

Or have you swallowed a wasp?

If you are unlucky and you swallow a wasp, put a teaspoon of salt in your mouth. This kills the wasp and heals the sting.

REMEDIES

How to help a cough or cold

Drink a cup of hot water with a spoonful of treacle before you go to bed.

Drink one cup of honey, half a cup of vinegar and some pepper (yuk!).

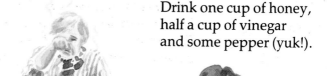

Put a sweaty sock around your throat at night!

We all know that we can eat onions but did you know that people used them . . .

to cure toothache? Put an onion skin on your big toe!

for earache? Hold a roast onion against your ear.

for a bald patch? Rub the patch with onion juice and honey. Your hair will grow again!

TRAINING
of a
CHAMPION

Edward the Hippopotamus is eight years old. He isn't very smart at school, but he *is* good at swimming. He's so good that his grandfather thinks there's a chance Edward could win the 27th Annual African Hippopotamus Race, which is to be held in six days time. Once, long ago, Grandfather Theodore came third in this race, so he tells Edward that he will be his trainer. But Edward's training programme is hard on Grandfather too!

Every morning, when it was still dark and ordinary hippopotamuses were still asleep, with the sky like velvet and the stars just starting to go out, Edward leapt from his bed, out of his pyjamas and into his bathing trunks.

Wasting not a second, looking to neither left nor right, he ran for the river at the end of the garden, and dived in.

Splash!

First he swam eight kilometres down the river, going as fast as he could. Then he flipped over and came all the way back, trying to go even faster. His little bulgy eyes were closed tight — except for an occasional fast look just to make sure he was going in the right direction — while his huge mouth was open one minute, closed the next, sucking up enormous breaths. Over and over went his arms, cleaving a pathway through the water. And with each stroke of an arm, he gave a powerful kick with a leg.

Whoosh! Whoosh!

And no sooner was he back at the garden than he immediately began twenty minutes of vigorous exercises, touching his toes, running on the spot, windmills, press-ups, deep knee bends and two-legged leaps.

And then, when that was done, Edward put on his dressing gown and sat down to breakfast with the rest of the family.

"How did it go, Champ?" Edward's father asked him. Ever since Edward had started training, his father had taken to calling him "Champ".

"Terrific!" Edward said. "I feel fine."

And how hungry he was after all that exercising. Six eggs! Four glasses of milk! Ten pieces of toast, each piece thickly buttered and covered with marmalade.

"Watch that diet, Champ," his father said.

"Quickly, now," said Edward's mother, "It's time for school."

And Edward had just enough time to change into his school clothes, grab his school bag, and run off.

Back he came at twelve o'clock, when school finished for the day, and hippopotamuses went home for lunch and to sleep in the afternoon — a very sensible thing to do when it's hot.

His grandfather allowed Edward only one hour's sleep — most hippopotamuses have three or four — and then training began again.

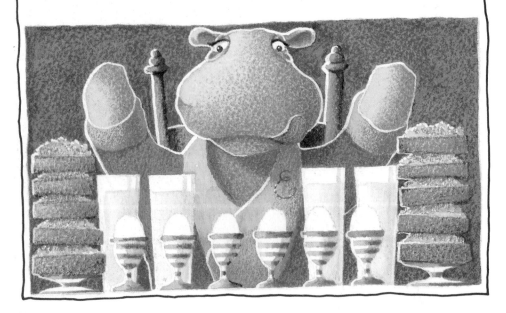

This time, when Edward dived into the river, his grandfather jumped on to a bicycle, and as Edward swam down the river, his grandfather bicycled along the bank, shouting out instructions through a megaphone.

"Keep your head down! Keep your head down! Use your legs! Use your legs!"

He shouted everything twice, because he knew it was hard to hear when you were swimming fast with your eyes shut tight and your mouth opening and closing, sucking up enormous quantities of air.

"Push with that left leg! Push with that left leg!" he shouted, his legs flying on the bicycle pedals.

"That'll do! That'll do! Come out! Come out! Take a rest. Whew! You're too fast for me."

Poor old Theodore. It was a long time since he'd done anything as strenuous as bicycling up and down a river bank, shouting instructions through a megaphone. He felt a bit wobbly in the legs.

"How's it going, Champ?" said Edward's father.

"Fine!" said Edward. "I feel terrific."

"He's too fast for me," said Edward's grandfather. "I'm out of breath. Just a minute. Lots to do. Lots to do. Lotssssss . . ."

Edward's grandfather was asleep.

But an hour later he was back again, as keen as ever.

"Now, Edward," he said, "back into the river. This time I'm going to time you with my stop watch. I want you to swim five kilometres, up to that tree, as fast as you can. Ready? On your marks! Go!"

That night, when Edward was in bed, fast asleep, Edward's grandfather sat down at the family desk, unscrewed his fountain pen, and, very carefully, wrote a letter to the President of the Twenty-Seventh Annual African Hippopotamus Race.

"Dear President," he wrote. "I would like to enter my grandson Edward in the Twenty-Seventh Annual African Hippopotamus Race. His vital statistics are as follows: he is one and a half metres high. He is three metres long. His weight is two and a half tonnes and two kilograms. His age: eight last birthday. I believe him to be a true champion, but that you will be able to judge for yourself. He is being trained by yours truly." And here he signed his name.
There!

And so the days went, each day beginning with the *buzz-buzz* of Edward's alarm clock.

Into the river!

And there was so much to learn.

One afternoon, Edward's grandfather began to show Edward how to do a proper racing dive.

"Head down! Head down!" he called. "On your marks! On your marks!"

Edward tucked his head down. Up went his arms. He hooked his toes over the edge of the riverbank, for extra leverage. He took a deep breath, and held it. He leant forward, and waited for the signal to dive in.

Seconds passed. Edward, tense as a spring, waited and waited. Where was the signal?

"Oh!" cried Edward, who could lean forward no longer, and before he could help himself, in he toppled.

Splash!

Up shot a huge wave of water, waking up Edward's grandfather.

"What happened?" said Edward's grandfather. "Oh dear, I fell asleep."

"Do you want me to try it again?" asked Edward.

"Um," said Edward's grandfather, who still felt sleepy. "No. This time I want you to swim eight kilometres down the river, and eight kilometres back. As fast as you can. Ready? Go!"

And while Edward was swimming down the river as fast as he could, Edward's grandfather took a nap under a shady tree. Edward's training really was taking it out of him. It was a long time since he had had to do so much.

Morris Lurie
Illustrated by *Gordon Fitchett*

What do you weigh?

Our weight is usually measured in pounds or kilograms. A hippopotamus's weight is usually given in tonnes!

In ancient times, people used grains of wheat or rice in order to work out how much something weighed. The Bible mentions "shekels"; a shekel was approximately the weight of 200 grains.

At some stage 480 grains was called an "ounce". There are 16 ounces in a pound. The word "pound" comes from the Latin word *pondus*, meaning "weight". One pound is almost half a kilogram. There are 1000 kilograms in a tonne.

(What does "ponderous" mean? How would you use it to describe someone?)

I'm 2½ tonnes. That's 2500 kilograms, or over 42 million grains! Gosh!

A kilogram equals one thousand grams.

And "gram" comes from the Greek word <u>gramma</u> which means "small weight."

Lizzie Dripping
and the Witch

Once upon a time, there was a girl called Lizzie Dripping. She walked about with her head in the clouds and was always trying to make life more exciting, more full of shivers, panics and laughter than it is if you leave it to itself.

Lizzie went up to the shop and bought some butter, and as she walked slowly back home down Kirk Street, she all of a sudden had the feeling that she would like a walk around the graveyard. And being Lizzie, it was no sooner thought than done. She scrambled up the bank by the memorial cross and next minute was through the little swing gate into the graveyard itself. She stopped dead.

You really could not believe your eyes. You could *not*, absolutely not, walk up your own street on a hot September afternoon, turn into the graveyard for a quiet half-hour, and see a witch sitting there.

Lizzie saw the witch before the witch saw her. What the witch was doing, was sitting with her back propped against a tombstone—the one in memory of *Hannah Post of this parish and Albert Cyril beloved husband of the above 1802 to 1879 Peace Perfect Peace*. Lizzie was not sure which shocked her most—seeing a witch at all, or seeing a witch propped against a tombstone.

Nobody should sit, lean or stand upon a tombstone. It showed disrespect for the dead. Lizzie herself sometimes did all three of these things, but never *carelessly*, as if it didn't matter. When *she* sat on a tombstone, it was with a thudding heart and a pounding sense of wickedness that would have made it quite impossible for her to do a single row of knitting or read so much as a page of a book.

And the witch was doing both. She sat in a black, untidy heap with a book propped open against a little marble flower pot that Lizzie was *sure* had been moved from the nearby grave of *Betsy Mabel Glossop aged 79 years Life's Work Well Done.*

Her hands, which were the only part of her that showed, kept making awkward jerking stabs with a pair of long wooden pins from which hung a length of lacy, soot-black knitting. Either it was lacy, or full of holes. Holes, probably, Lizzie decided. The witch did not look at all a good knitter.

The longer she stood there, the more Lizzie wondered whether she was actually seeing what she seemed to be seeing. She closed her eyes for a moment, then opened them again. She saw the crooked stones, green with moss, she saw the tall cow parsley with its seeding heads, she saw the roof of Pond Farm in the dip below. And she saw a black bundle topped with a pointed hat propped against the tombstone of the Perfectly Peaceful Posts. She saw a witch.

Lizzie turned and went softly back along the little path by the church, through the gate and back into Kirk Street, hot and shadowless and smelling of the blue smoke from the burning stubble. No one was about except Jake Staples, who was not really worth talking to. He was playing marbles with himself outside his house. Lizzie stood over him for a minute, watching him cheat.

"Hello," she said. "Who's winning?"

"Me," said Jake.

It struck Lizzie that perhaps Jake was the one person in Little Hemlock who would believe there was a witch in the churchyard. After all, he had believed her the time she had told him his house was on fire. He had left off knocking conkers down from Mrs Adams's chestnut and gone running down the village like ten furies. (Leaving Lizzie, who often had a reason for fibbing to pick up his pile of conkers and stow them in her own bag.)

"There's a witch in the graveyard," she told him now.

"And pigs can fly," replied Jake, killing two marbles in one go. "Cats've got five legs. Monkeys are bl–" (He was going to say "blue".)

"I tell you there is" she said.

"You go away, Lizzie Dripping," said Jake. "I'm busy."

"And don't you dare call me that!" she cried.

"Everyone else does. Lizzie Dripping! My ma says you're a fibber and I'm not to talk to you."

"You say that once more," said Lizzie, "and I'll kick your marbles flying. I'll kick them to the four corners of the earth!"

She liked saying that, because she knew for a fact that the earth was round and didn't *have* any corners. Jake began to pick his marbles up and stuff them rapidly into his pockets.

"I'm going to tell my ma about you," he said.

"And I'm going to tell that witch about you!" returned Lizzie.

She marched back towards the church. Once out of sight and past the gate, she tiptoed. It was one thing to see a witch, and quite another to let a witch see you.

There she still sat, in a great black hunch. Lizzie stepped off the path behind a particularly large, show-off slab in memory of one of *The Petersons of the Manor*. The soft buff plumes of seeding grass brushed her bare legs.

"I spy with my little eye!" said a voice.

Lizzie leapt and banged her knee hard against the stone.

"Owch!"

"Saw you the first time, and I see you now," came the same cracked, chatty voice. The fingers were still stabbing with the needles, the face still hidden under that wide black brim.

Lizzie stood poised. Should she run or should she stay? She wanted, despite the knocking of her knees and the thudding of her heart, to stay. She knew for a fact that in all Little Hemlock there was no one half so interesting to talk to as this witch.

"If *I* was going to hide," the voice went on, "I should vanish into thin air."

Lizzie stepped from behind the stone.

"What, knitting and all?" she asked, interested.

For an answer, the witch vanished. Lizzie blinked. She could still smell clover and nettles, and the pigeons were still crooning in the yews, and at the far end of the village she could hear the chimes of the ice-cream van.

"I am definitely awake," she said to herself, and as if to prove it, stepped sideways and stung her leg on a nettle.

"Owch!" she cried again, rubbing it.

"So that's that," she said out loud at last. "Seeing one of my own fibs, I expect."

Lizzie was a very *honest* fibber.

Then the witch was there again, still knitting.

"You *are* there!" cried Lizzie.

"Knit one, slip one, knit one, pass the slip stitch over," said the witch. "Of course I am. And I'm fed up with knitting. Fiddling, baby clothes is. Fiddle fiddle fiddle."

She plunged the spare needle fiercely into the black cobweb, fished for the ball of wool, and stowed them all into a pocket somewhere in her black robes.

"The thing is," said Lizzie, choosing her words carefully. "There are no such things as witches."

"That's all right, then, isn't it?" said the witch. "Come a little closer, and I'll turn you into a toad."

Lizzie let out a little squeal and clapped her hand to her mouth.

"I'm sorry!" she cried. "I didn't mean to be rude!"

The witch looked up then. Her face certainly looked like what a witch's face would look like if there were such things as witches.

"Try me," she said.

"T-try you?" repeated Lizzie.

"Tell me something to do. A test."

"You mean a *spell*?"

Lizzie felt a swift shiver under the hot sun. Could a spell happen in Little Hemlock, on her own doorstep?

"I...I don't know if I want to, actually, thank you," she said at last.

"Rubbish!" snapped the witch. "You're dying to, girl!"

It was true. The fibbing part of Lizzie, the part of her that wanted to believe in everything and anything under the sun, was itching. It was itching to see the impossible actually *happen*.

"Come along," said the witch. "I haven't got all day."

"Just a minute," said Lizzie. "Let me think."

Quick. Think. Blank. Nothing. The best fibber in Little Hemlock stuck for an idea. Lizzie Dripping, of all people!

"In a minute," said the witch, beginning to sound dangerous, "*I* shall think of something."

"Oh! Oh dear!" Lizzie was frantic. "What about ... what about ...?"

She was hedging for time.

"What about what?" inquired the witch relentlessly.

"What-about-turning-that-bird-into-a-toad?"

It all came out in a rush. She didn't feel herself *think* it, only heard herself *say* it. Somewhere at the back of her mind she had the idea that witches specialised in turning things into toads. And if anything round here was going to be turned into a toad, she didn't want to be it.

"What? Is that all?" The witch sounded disappointed.

"Which bird?" She scanned about her with eyes that looked oddly short-sighted for a witch. As if reading Lizzie's thoughts (and a chill ran down Lizzie's back), she dug into her robes and fished out a pair of spectacles.

"Which bird?" she repeated, looking about her over the rims.

"Th ... that one!" Lizzie really did not care. She picked on an unsuspecting thrush sitting halfway up a yew that hung over the grave of Robert Miller (*Come Unto Me All Ye That Labour*).

"Poor thrush!" she thought fleetingly, just in time to see it turn toad. She clapped a hand to her mouth.

"Hmmmm!" she heard the witch's mutter. "Not much to *that*. Any more?"

She picked on a robin, worming by a granite cross.

"Oh!" Lizzie gasped again. "Poor robin!"

There were two toads now. One by the cross and one halfway up the yew. The one in the yew looked startled, even for a toad.

"Oh! Turn them back, can't you?" she cried. "Look at that poor thing up the tree — oooh! Look out — it's going to jump!"

It did, too. And what was even more surprising, landed safely. It certainly looked bewildered, staring out among the grasses on the grave of Robert Miller (*Come Unto Me All Ye That Labour*), but more at home than up in the tree.

"'T' ain't nature, toads in trees," remarked the witch.

"For all the world," thought Lizzie, "as if turning birds into toads *was* nature!"

"Now what?" asked the witch impatiently.

33

"Now she's started spelling," thought Lizzie, "how on earth am I going to stop her?"

Desperately she racked her brains for something interesting but *safe*. After all, the witch had turned the birds *into* toads, but there was no guarantee at all that she would — or even could — turn them back again.

"P'raps I'd better find out," she thought.

"What about turning them back?" she suggested.

The witch looked disappointed.

"Back? Already? Bird to toad, toad to bird? Child's play. Waste a witch's time, would you?"

Sulkily she snapped her fingers again and muttered under her breath. Next minute the two surprised-looking toads were two surprised-looking birds. They flew off — right off and on out of sight. Lizzie watched them go — and hardly blamed them.

"Now what?" said the witch again. "And not toads, this time."

Lizzie's brain went blank again. Quick. Think.

"Don't believe in me, girl, do ye?" snapped the witch. "*I* know, *I* can tell."

"Of — c-course I do!"

The witch sniffed.

"*My* turn, any hows," she said. "Turn and turn about. *My* turn to choose a spell."

"Oh...oh dear! All right, then!" cried Lizzie a little desperately. She crossed her fingers, on both hands.

"Now you see one!" cried the witch. "And now you see *three*!"

"Oooooh!" Lizzie let out a shrill squeal. Facing her in a row, like ravens on a bough, were *three* witches! Lizzie blinked rapidly, in case there was something in her eye that was making her see treble. But there was no doubt about it at all. Propped against the tombstone of the Perfectly Peaceful Posts were three definite, distinct witches.

Her own witch—the one in the middle—looked pleased.

"That's more like home," she remarked. "And three can spell easier than one, eh, girls?"

The other two cackled merrily.

"If all three of them do *that* spell," thought Lizzie in a panic, "then there'll be *nine* witches. And if *they* all do it, there'll be twenty-seven, and if *they* all do it, there'll be..." but her arithmetic gave out. Instead of a number, all she came up with was a terrible picture of Little Hemlock churchyard thick with spelling witches—*blackened* with them.

Lizzie was desperate. Her mother had told her time and again that she should never speak to strangers. But why, oh *why*, had she not warned her never, ever, to speak to witches?

"*Now* do you believe in witches?" cried Lizzie's witch triumphantly.

"I do! I do!" Lizzie cried. "I believed in you before, really I did! But now I believe in you *three* times as much! Honestly! Really!"

"Well, then," said the witch, "give us a spell to do. A proper one, this time. Come along, girl."

Lizzie Dripping's brain turned to water again. What should she say? Change the church into a gingerbread palace…? No. Put bags of potato crisps instead of daisies…? Better…Make her own hair grow down to her waist and be buttercup yellow instead of brown? *That* was it! Just as she'd always dreamed—two lovely long pigtails, long as Rapunzel's—or at least, long enough to sit on. She would tie them with scarlet ribbons and parade up and down the Main Street. Wouldn't they all stare …?

"I've thought!" she cried, "I've got a spell for you! Make my hair…"

But she never finished.

"Lizzie Dripping! Lizzie Dripping!"

She turned quickly. It was Jake Staples, there by the gate.

"Thought you said there was a witch!" he yelled. "Witch my foot. Witch my elbow! Witch yourself!

Lizzie Dripping, Lizzie Dripping,
Don't look now, your fibs are slipping!
Lizzie Dripping, Lizzie Dripping,
Don't…"

"Go away!" she screamed. "Go away this minute! You'll spoil..."

She turned back to where the witches were, and stopped dead.

"Oooooh!" She let out her breath in a long gasp. Where the witches were—the witches weren't.

Gone. Vanished—as only witches *can* vanish. From one moment to the next, into thin air...

Written by Helen Cresswell,
illustrated by Bryna Waldman

Odd inscriptions on tombstones

If you look in any churchyard, you will find many interesting and, perhaps, odd inscriptions on the tombstones. Here are a few, from England and America.

FANCY THAT

Solomon Peas

Peas is not here,
Only the pod.
Peas shelled out
Went home to God.

(Ruidosa,
New Mexico,
USA)

Here as ever sleeping sound,
Lies our Julie in the ground.
If she wake, as wake she may,
There'll be fun on judgement day.

(Oswestry, Shropshire, England)

John Penny

Reader, if cash thou art
in want of any,
Dig four feet down
and find a Penny.

(Wimborne,
Dorset,
England)

Here lies John Yeast.
Pardon me for not rising.

Here lies shoot-em-up Jake.
Run for sheriff in 1872.
Run from sheriff in 1876.
Buried 1876.

(Dodge City, Kansas, USA)

R.I.P.

I put my wife
Beneath this stone
For her repose
And for my OWN.

(Middlebury,
Vermont, USA)

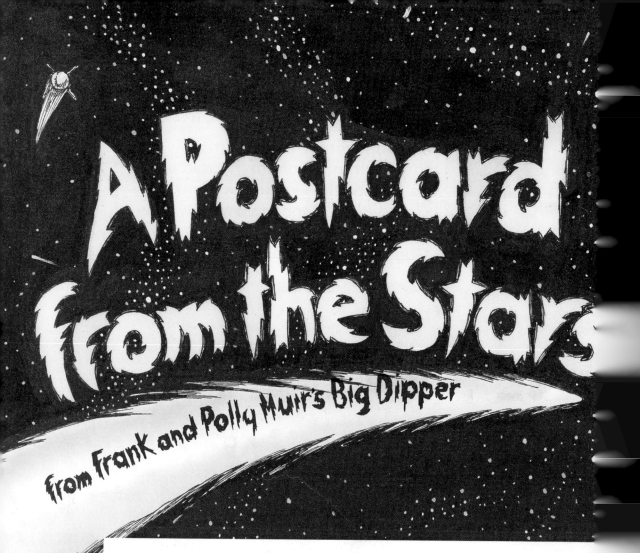

A Postcard from the Stars

from Frank and Polly Muir's Big Dipper

"What are you going to do with that pile of junk?" Liam called when his brother got back from the scrap-yard with the old Lambretta.

"Rebuild it like new," said Jack proudly. Then he glared at Liam. "And if you lay a finger on it, you'll need rebuilding!"

"I bet they paid you to take it away," Liam shouted from the safety of the fence. "Who'd want to play with that prehistoric wreck!"

He did, of course, so when everyone had gone to bed he put on his dressing-gown and borrowed Jack's gauntlets and crash helmet and crept out into the garden and sat on the Lambretta.

It was very quiet out there, very quiet and very dark.

"Waaaaarrrrr-waaaaarrrrr—thrummmm!" Liam murmured softly as he took the lead in the Manx Grand Prix. "Poooooowwwwwwwwww—Zzzzowwwwwww—Gggggggrrmmmmmmmggggggg!"

He was changing gear for the tight bend before the home straight.

"Zzzzowwwwwwww!" he whispered.

"Ggrukk," something answered.

Liam almost leapt off the seat.

"I didn't say that!"

"Ggrukkk," it went again.

"I didn't say that either!"

But something had!

Liam's hair began to stand up straight under the crash-helmet, and he could feel little prickles down his back. He wanted to jump off the Lambretta and make a run for his warm bed, but he didn't dare move.

What if the thing that went "Ggrukk!" was waiting for him?

What if it saw him as he ran for the kitchen?

"I'm not moving!" Liam whispered to himself. "I'll sit here till I'm sure it's gone, then I'll run like an Olympic champion for the back door and maybe it won't get me!"

So Liam sat very still and he waited.

And he waited.

And he waited some more.

"It's gone," he told himself.

He listened again.

"Has it gone?"

He was just about to jump off the old motor-scooter and hare for the kitchen when a metallic sort of grumpy noise went "Grukkk!"

"It's there again!" Liam said to himself. "I wish I was in bed! I wish I hadn't come out to see Jack's rotten old scooter! I wish I hadn't sat on it! I wish I hadn't started yelling 'Warrrrrthrummmm' and all those other daft noises!"

He wished so hard he almost thought he hadn't done any of these things, and he was so good at wishing they hadn't happened that he thought he really was back in his own room, at least until something else happened to tell him he wasn't.

And what happened was this:

Behind him — yes, exactly behind him, and a bit below where he was sitting — something went "Grukkk".

"Oooohh!" Liam cried out aloud.

"Grukkk!" went the noise behind him again, and this time the motor-scooter shook a little — just a little, but enough for Liam to know that there definitely was something behind him, and a little below him.

"It's here!" wailed Liam. "It's in the Lambretta!"

"Gress grri grram!" it answered.

"It's a ghost!" Liam wailed.

"Grro grri'm grrot," it said.

"It's a ghost with a cold!" wailed Liam.

"Grri'm grrot a ghrosstt!" it said impatiently.

"It's a ghost with a cold and it's right behind me," said Liam, who was badly scared, though he wasn't too scared to ask himself what sort of a ghost with a cold went out haunting people on old motor-scooters.

So, though he was scared, he looked around, where, down below him, was the engine, right under the seat of the Lambretta, and the engine was glowing with an odd sort of pearly glow!

"It's in the engine!" Liam said. "It's a ghost with a bad cold right in our Jack's old scooter. What's it doing there?"

"Grrying gro gggret groutt!" it answered in a very angry tone of voice.

"Grying gro grret groutt?" Liam repeated. "Ggrying gro gret groutt? What sort of talk is that?"

"Ggrenglish!" it yelled.

"Ggrenglish?" pondered Liam. "Grott's Ggrenglish?" Then he understood, because he was talking in the same way as the ghost. "You're talking English with too many g's ghostie!" he said. "Anyway, what are you doing down there?"

"Ggrying gro gret groutt!"

"I know!" said Liam. "Trying to get out. You must be stuck in the sump, ghostie. I'll get some oil and maybe that'll ease your throat a bit. Hang around!"

Liam was still a bit scared, but he was too interested to run for the kitchen now and miss the fun. He couldn't be scared of a ghost who was stuck in an old scooter, could he?

No, he told himself, he couldn't.

He poured oil into the engine, and the pearly glow increased.

"How are you doing in there?" he said. "Feel better, ghostie?"

There was a long oily gurgling sound.

"Ah. Aah! Better. Better and better! And don't call me ghostie, I'm not a ghost."

44

"Well, what are you?" asked Liam.

"I'm what I suppose you'd call an alien, since I'm not from your planet," the creature, or whatever it was, said.

"Get off with you," said Liam faintly. He only said it because his mother said "Get off with you" when she was feeling peculiar.

"You can't be an alien. Aliens don't live in old Lambretta engines."

"It isn't my usual abode, I agree. But since my starship crashed on your planet—"

"—what!" interrupted Liam.

"I said, since my starship crashed near here and was taken to a junkyard and crushed up for scrap, I've had to survive wherever I can."

"In an engine?" said Liam.

"That's where we live," said the creature. "Right amongst the explosions. We're most comfortable where it's hot and cramped and where there's a lot of noise. I needed a place to live when my starship went for scrap, so I transferred to this contraption when they brought it to the junkyard, and there I stayed, getting colder every day, until that brother of yours bought the Lambretta and brought it back here."

"How much did Jack pay?" said Liam.

"Five pounds!" growled the creature, and its pearly glow went red. "Five pounds for an old motor-scooter and for me, Grok of the famous race of Grokkles!"

Liam's head was spinning. He wasn't afraid any more but how could he explain to Jack, or to his mum, that the Lambretta contained a stranded star-traveller who glowed in the dark and was called Grok?

"I don't know what we're going to do about this, Grok," he said. "Can't you come out of there?"

"No!" said Grok. "Grokkles live in engines! We thrive best in a nice warm million degree fission engine, but even an ancient relic like this is better than nothing, and the sooner this one starts up, the sooner I can get away!"

"But where to?" said Liam. "You won't get far on this old wreck."

"This old wreck can take us right back to my home star, Grokkle-Bright," said Grok. "Just pass me the Lambretta manual and fill up the tank, and I'll show you a thing or two!"

"Will you?" said Liam.

"Sure!" Grok told him.

"Like what?" said Liam.

"Like a tour round a couple of galaxies." said Grok.

"On Jack's Lambretta?"

"Sure!"

Liam laughed with amazement and delight. The Manx Grand Prix could manage without him now.

"O.K., Grok!"

In a couple of minutes, Grok glowed blue then red then pearly-white while he studied the Lambretta manual, as Liam filled the tank with the petrol-and-oil mixture.

46

"Ready?" said Liam.

"Nearly," Grok told him.

"How do we get out into space?" said Liam.

"Just a minute," said Grok.

Liam looked back at the house, wondering if he had been missed yet.

"Are you sure about trips round galaxies on the Lambretta?" he asked nervously.

"Give me time," said Grok.

But there wasn't any more time.

From the bedroom over the kitchen came a huge yell.

"Where's Liam!" bellowed Jack.

"What's that noise?" said Grok.

"Jack," said Liam faintly. "He's gone to bed."

"Does he always bellow like that in bed?" said Grok.

"Only when he's mad with me," said Liam.

"Aaaargh!" bellowed Jack. "I'll demolish him!"

"Oh," moaned Liam.

"Be quiet!" said Grok.

"Hurry up!" Liam yelled.

The back door burst open, and the garden was suddenly full of bright light.

"There he is!" bawled Jack. "He's on my Lambretta! And he's got my gear on!"

"Careful, Liam," warned Liam's mum. "Jack isn't very pleased with you."

"What do we do now?" moaned Liam.

"Kick the kick-start," said Grok.

Jack was rushing towards him, though, and Liam was too terrified to move, and if Jack hadn't fallen over the oilcan where Liam had left it on the grass, Jack might really have carried out his threat, and then Liam would never have got the Lambretta to start, but Jack *did* fall —very heavily!

"What are you doing, Jack?" called his mother.

"Falling down!" roared Jack.

Liam breathed a sigh of relief and kicked the kick-start.

The old Lambretta roared into louder life than it had ever done before, and Jack said later that it sounded more like a rocket engine than a motor-scooter.

"Off we go," said Grok, "Into gear!"

Liam snapped the gear-lever.

"Powwwwww—zoooommmmmmm!" howled the Lambretta.

"Where to?" yelled Liam above the noise.

A flash of moonlight came from behind the clouds.

"Straight up the moonbeam," said Grok.

So Liam pointed the Lambretta for the moonlight, and to the absolute astonishment of Jack, and Jack's mum, and his dad, who had just come out to see what all the noise was about, Liam and the Lambretta zoomed up into the sky along a bright, white moonbeam with a noise like an interstellar ship.

"What's that boy up to now?" said Liam's dad.

"I'll send you a postcard!" Liam called down to his family. "'Bye!"

"A postcard?" said Liam's dad. "He'll have a job getting it delivered from up there."

Liam's mum thought otherwise.

"Liam always keeps his promises," she said. "If he says he'll send a postcard, he'll send it."

So Liam's mum and dad, and Jack too, now that he'd got over losing his Lambretta, watched the sky every night, and after a week they saw what they were looking for.

In the gap between the constellations of Orion and the Pleiades, a new set of stars had appeared, and together they spelt out a message:

Having a lovely time—wish you were here—
back soon—love Liam.

Brian Ball
Illustrated by
Gaston Vanzet

51

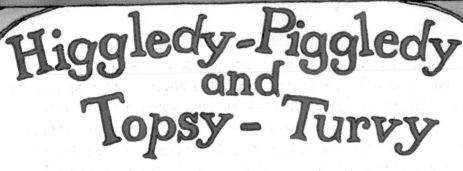

Higgledy-Piggledy and Topsy-Turvy

Once upon a time there was a very busy woman. She was busy all day long because she had so much to do. She had the beds to make, and the floors to scrub, and jerseys to knit, and the sheets to mend on the sewing-machine, and the clothes to iron — oh, and ever so many things more. And one day she felt just plain tired of working, and she said out loud, "I can't manage any longer by myself. I wish I had someone to help me."

No sooner had she said this than there was a knock at the front door. She opened it and there was a little old woman. And the little old woman said,

> "Ask me in,
> Ask me inner,
> I'll help you
> If you give me dinner."

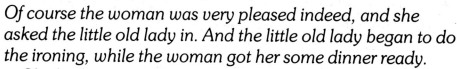

Of course the woman was very pleased indeed, and she asked the little old lady in. And the little old lady began to do the ironing, while the woman got her some dinner ready.

She had just put the meat in the pan to cook when there was another knock at the door. She opened it and there was another little old woman. And this little old woman said,

"Ask me in,
Ask me inner,
I'll help you
If you give me dinner."

So then the woman was even more pleased, and she asked the little old woman in. The little old woman began to scrub the floor, while she put some more carrots with the meat to make more dinner.

She had scarcely done this when
there was another knock at the door, and
there was another little old woman. And she said, just
like the other two,

"Ask me in,
Ask me inner,
I'll help you
If you give me dinner."

The woman was beginning to get a bit bothered by now, but
she asked her in the same as the others, and put more
onions with the meat to make more dinner. And the
little old woman began to mend the sheets on
the sewing-machine.

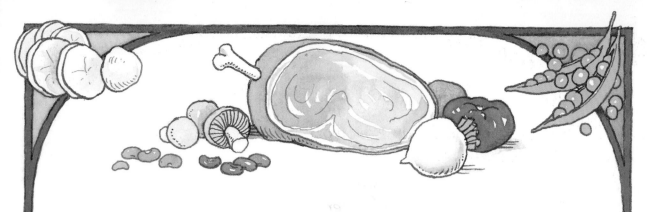

The woman had scarcely put the onions in when there was another knock at the door. And so it went on, more and more little old ladies coming to the door, and every one saying,

"Ask me in,
Ask me inner,
I'll help you
If you give me dinner."

And now they didn't even wait to be asked to come in. They came in themselves, and they started work, one making the beds, one knitting jerseys, one doing one thing, one doing another, and eating, eating, all the time. All the time they were working they were eating, and the more the woman cooked for them and the more she baked for them, the hungrier they seemed to get. And at last she was so hot and bothered that she didn't know what to do.

So she went to her husband who was asleep in bed all this time, the lucky man, and she tried to wake him up to come and help her. She shook him and she shouted in his ear, but it was no use, he just wouldn't wake up.

So she put on her hat and coat, and she went to see a wise woman who lived over the hill, and left all the little old women eating and working away, with some more bread baking in the oven.

She told the wise woman all about it, and asked her what she should do. "First of all," said the wise woman, "don't ever say again you can't manage by yourself. And secondly, just go home now and when you get to your doorstep, stand there and shout 'The hill's on fire!' Then all the little old women will come dashing out to have a look, and you must shut the door quickly, and as fast as you can, make everything higgledy-piggledy, topsy-turvy, upside-down and inside out and as tingle-tangled as can be. And last of all wake up your husband by splashing some water on his face."

So the woman thanked her and hurried away.

As soon as she got to her own doorstep, she stood there and shouted out "The hill's on fire!" And all the little old women came running out to see. And the woman quickly shut the door and started to make everything in the house higgledy-piggledy, topsy-turvy, upside-down and inside out and as tingle-tangled as could be. She turned the sewing-machine upside-down, she put the pillow at the bottom of the bed instead of at the top, she took the handle off the top of the bucket and fastened it to the bottom, she turned the clothes that were being ironed all inside out, she took the needles out of the knitting and stuck them somewhere else, and tangled the wool into knots just as if a kitten had been playing with it.

Then all the little old women outside the door began to bang and shout, "Let us in, let us in!"

"The hill's on fire!"

"I can't," said the woman. "I'm busy. I'm baking bread."

"Bucket, come and open the door!" they shouted.

"I can't," said the bucket. "My handle's on the wrong end. I'm all upside-down."

"Sewing-machine, open the door!" they shouted.

"I can't," said the sewing-machine. "I'm the wrong way up. I'm all topsy-turvy."

"Bed, come and open the door!" they shouted.

"I can't," said the bed. "My pillow's at the bottom end. I'm all higgledy-piggledy."

"Clothes, come and open the door," they shouted.

"We can't," said the clothes. "We're all inside out."

"Knitting, open the door!" they shouted.

"I can't. My needles are stuck in the wrong place and I'm all tingle-tangled."

Then the little old women remembered the bread that was baking in the oven.

"Bread, come and open the door," they shouted.

And the bread got out of the oven and was just going to open the door for them, when the woman grabbed the bread knife and quickly cut it into slices.

Then she remembered what to do about the water. She took a cupful from the tap, and threw it over her husband who was still snoring away. He woke up in a flash, and he dashed to the door where the little old women were banging and shouting, and he shouted in a voice like thunder, "Go away!" And they did!

Leila Berg
Illustrated by *Cindy Hunnam*

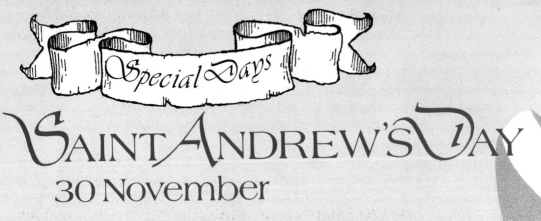

Saint Andrew's Day

30 November

Who was Saint Andrew?

Andrew was one of Christ's Apostles. The Bible tells us he came from the city of Bethsaida. Both Andrew and his brother Peter were fishermen, but they gave up their jobs so they could follow Jesus.

Why is he remembered?

Like the other disciples, Andrew lived and worked with Jesus. Once Jesus was crucified, the disciples became preachers and they spent the rest of their lives working for Christianity.

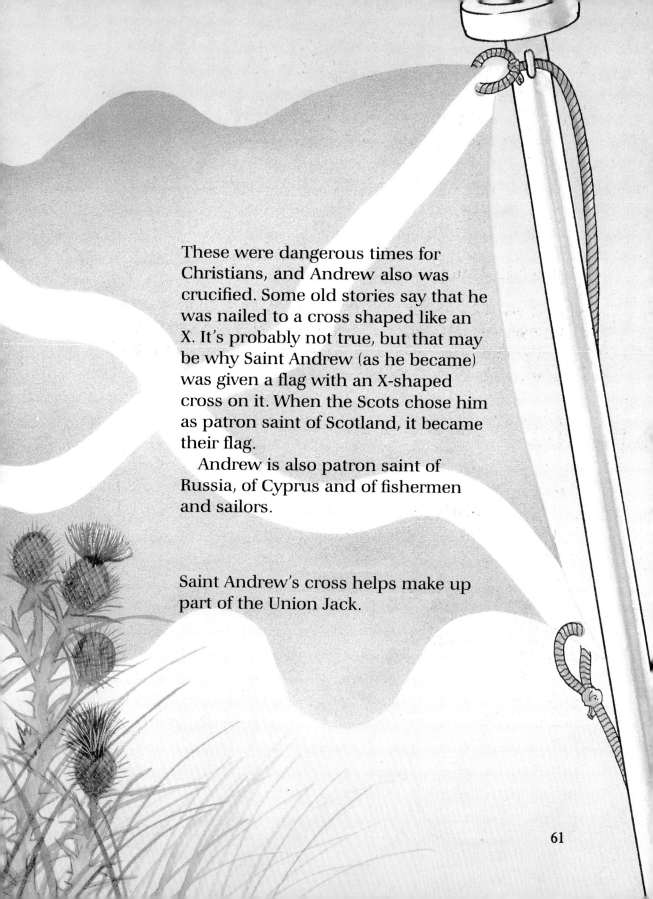

These were dangerous times for Christians, and Andrew also was crucified. Some old stories say that he was nailed to a cross shaped like an X. It's probably not true, but that may be why Saint Andrew (as he became) was given a flag with an X-shaped cross on it. When the Scots chose him as patron saint of Scotland, it became their flag.

Andrew is also patron saint of Russia, of Cyprus and of fishermen and sailors.

Saint Andrew's cross helps make up part of the Union Jack.

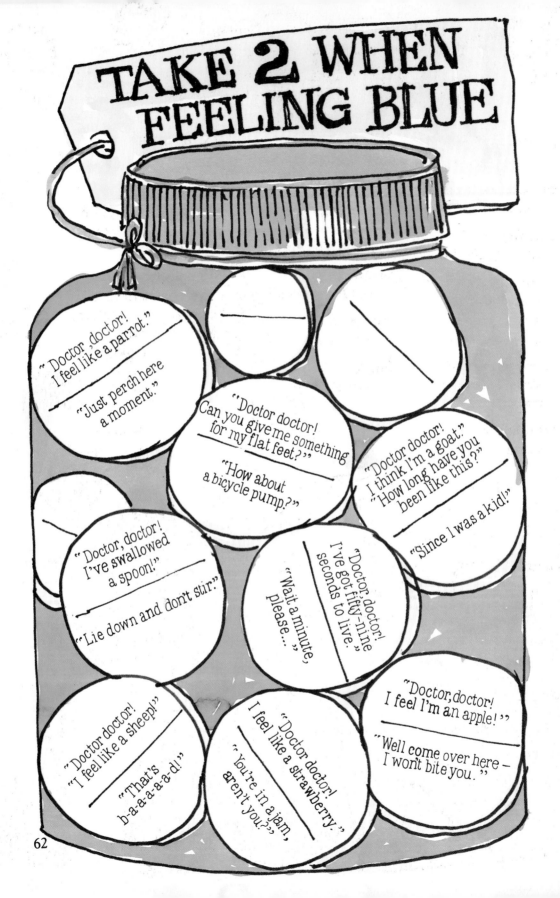

A MARVELLOUS MIX OF WORDS

Glossary

abode (*p. 45*)
home

bewildered (*p. 33*)
confused

cleaving (*p. 19*)
cutting; dividing

constellations (*p. 50*)
stars that appear
grouped; they
usually have names

contraption (*p. 45*)
strange-looking
machine

crooning (*p. 30*)
singing

demolish (*p. 49*)
to destroy, or
pull down

fission engine (*p. 46*)
an engine that
uses nuclear power

fleetingly (*p. 33*)
for only a second

forlorn (*p. 5*)
miserable

foul (*p. 11*)
horrible

frantic (*p. 32*)
excited; or anxious

galaxies (*p. 46*)
groups of connected
stars that make up
the universe

gauntlets (*p. 39*)
special leather
gloves to protect
the hands

Glossary
continues on
page 64

63

gleefully (p. 11)
very happily

granite (p. 33)
a hard type of
grey rock

hag (p. 7)
ugly old woman

hare for (p. 41)
to run fast like
a hare

hedging (p. 32)
making time to think

home straight (p. 41)
the straight part at
the end of a race
track, just before
the winning post

horny (p. 7)
hard and rough

hugely (p. 8)
widely

interstellar (p. 50)
travels between stars

Lambretta (p. 39)
a type of motor scooter

leverage (p. 24)
power — he would get
an extra push by using
his toes like a lever

Manx Grand Prix (p. 40)
a special race held
on the Isle of Man

memorial (p. 26)
a stone cross put up
in memory of someone

metallic (p. 41)
of or like metal

no guarantee (p. 34)
it was not certain

plumes (p. 30)
feathers; or shape
of feathers

poised (p. 30)
ready

prehistoric (p. 39)
ancient; before
history was written

pulp (p. 13)
a soft liquid mass

relentlessly (p. 32)
to not give up — she
keeps on asking

relic (p. 46)
something very old

repose (p. 38)
rest; sleep

strenuous (p. 22)
takes a lot of effort

striding (p. 6)
walking quickly with
long steps

sump (p. 44)
the part of an engine
that holds oil

unsuspecting (p. 32)
not to know what's
going on

worming (p. 33)
hunting for worms

yews (p. 30)
a type of tree with
small red berries

**"You've cooked the
old girl's goose"** (p. 9)
"You've finished
her off!"